The Collins Christian Co.

LCCN: 2021909303

Publication Data: 06/17/2021

Printed in the United States of America.

ISBN - 978-057891225-7

Editing: Aretta Raines

Pagination: Zanetta L. Collins

Cover: Zakaria Nada **www.behance.net/zakarianad**

Images: Mrahphotography

Make Up: Stamped By Quinn

Hair: Cynthia Freeman, Exquisite Hair & Replacement

Stylist: Zanetta L. Collins

ZANETTA CO

D1236866

DEDICATION

Mr. De'Vyon Amir-Malik

"Mighty King" Collins, last year the

most precious thing that I had and what

I valued the most was stripped from

me...you! I understand it looking

through our Father's eyes, but I am not

sure if I will ever be able to completely

grasp the totality of the situation with

my natural eyes! I DEFINITELY lost a

piece of my being... a piece of my soul

when I lost you! But yet will I trust Him!

God has given me the strength to continue pressing towards the mark, even though it hasn't been easy. Just know this, I did my best to be a positive example in your life and I choose to continue being an example in your death! I love you with every fiber of my being!

Always, your mother Zanetta…

ABOUT

Zanetta L. Collins was born to Valerie and Luther Collins Jr. in Fort Ord, California. Growing up with plenty of turbulent times, Zanetta through sports and sheer determination made it out of her hometown and attend college on a basketball scholarship. Zanetta shined as an athlete and used sports as her gateway to a better education and a brighter future.

However, during her journey,
the residue of her past caused her to
suffer from depression, anxiety,
borderline alcoholism, and
homosexuality.

While striving to obtain a college
degree, she encountered additional
obstacles and setbacks and during the
process, she gave birth to a beautiful
son, De'Vyon Amir-Malik Collins. Due
to sheer determination, after five years,
she obtained her AA Degree in

Communications from Eastern Florida

College in Cocoa, FL & a BA degree in

Psychology from Edward Waters

College in Jacksonville, Florida. Even

with a degree, she found it challenging

to find stable employment to provide

for her son.

Shortly after graduation, Zanetta

enlisted in the United States Army.

Once enlisted, she encountered

additional challenges with her health

and these medical issues forced her to

be medically discharged. After she had

been back in her hometown in Cocoa,

Florida for several years, the "real

journey" began when she accepted the

Lord as her personal Savior on August

18, 2009. This was undoubtedly the best

decision she had ever made. It was not

until this time that Zanetta began the

journey of discovering her identity and

to whom she belonged.

After giving her life to Christ,

Zanetta continued a quest for self-improvement and empowerment by

attending cosmetology school and

became a licensed cosmetologist. With a

spirit of entrepreneurship on her life,

Zanetta felt led to establish new

company entitled ZLC, Incorporated.

Within the last seven years,

Zanetta has published three additional

literary works, two of which were

published under her own publishing

company, The Collins Christian

Company entitled "The Colors of My

Wings" and "Once Broken." She also published "The Weight in the Wait" with Trilogy Publishing which is a subsidiary of the TNB Network. Additionally, Zanetta's company published "Silence Her No More" by Authoress Constance Burrell, and she works with other authors to create their own content.

In March of 2021, Zanetta also launched her first podcast entitled, "Walk by Faith" Podcast, which is geared towards spreading the gospel of

Jesus Christ and recounting how often

God has required us to walk by faith

and not by sight!

Forward

Reading what Zanetta writes always amazes me as well as encourages me as a leader. Week after week she sits in service...worshipping, receiving, many times not like those around her. There are times that she will make her way to the altar, for an exchange, agreement or simply strength to remain on "the Potter's wheel."

You never see the depth of impartation of faith; but it's always evident it in her books. I found value in reading, "The Potter's Wheel" because it is written from a relational viewpoint.

We all have struggles but the brunt of Zanetta's have seemed to stem from relational issues. Which makes this book more of a victory lap that the reader can participate in. To endure the loss of an only child, the struggle of justice while all eyes are on you was captured. It's transparent and embraces the power of a surrendered heart. That even in trauma, weariness, disappointment and the deafening screams of injustice...WHY, HOW, WHAT'S THE POINT...submitting to Christ will lead to peace, victory and a seat at the Masters table. If you want to witness, agree with or be led by example how to take the enemies weapons and turning them into tools for victory, the harvest of souls and Kingdom example...this is the book! It's a demonstration of all of Romans 8!

Apostle Shauna K. Jackson

TABLE OF CONTENTS

INTRODUCTION

I have learned that in my walk with Christ, God always starts with doing his best to perfect His creation. Not that we will ever be perfect but He's constantly shaping us, molding us, pushing us to be the best version of ourselves that we could possibly be in Christ! In my last book, "The Weight in the Wait" God cracked open this vessel and unfinished work began to spew out onto the pages. Some things I knew were there, but thinking they were non-

issues and some things that I didn't

even know were inside of me that

needed to be addressed and purged in

order to move from glory to glory! For

example, in "The Weight in the Wait"

God began dealing with me about

generational curses, unforgiveness,

judgment, unconditional love, and

forgiveness just to name a few.

In that book, one of the topics

was my son, De'Vyon Amir-Malik

Collins. At the time, my son even

though despite all odds had graduated

high school and was headed to college

to play football. Despite these blessings,

my son had a war ragging on the inside

and he was literally spiraling out of

control. His social circle changed, and

he started to exhibit behaviors that did

not align with his goals in life. These

changes were extremely unsettling to

me. Frankly, I think it would have been

unsettling to any parent, especially a mother.

Three months into 2020, I was given a prophetic release about my son and the word was basically that my son was going to be ok! It brought me some sense of relief. Despite what my natural eyes were seeing, I locked into the word that had been released. I also did what I was taught as a Christian to do, which was to stand on God's word and pray...

1

The Prayer of Supplication (Palal)

Prayer became a way that I went into battle for my son. I sat down and mapped out my strategic line of defense to help save my son, my boy! I went to two books, "*Prayers that Rout Demons*" and *"Uprooting the Spirit of Rejection."* Then I put on *"the full armor of God."*

A final word:

Be strong in the Lord and in his mighty power. Put on all of God's armor so that you will be able to stand firm against all strategies of the devil. For we[a] are not fighting against flesh-and-blood enemies, but against evil rulers and authorities of the unseen world, against mighty powers in this dark world, and against evil spirits in the heavenly places. Therefore, put on every piece of God's armor so you will be able to resist the enemy in the time of evil. Then after the battle, you will still be standing firm. Stand your ground, putting on the belt of truth and the body armor of God's righteousness. For shoes, put on the peace that comes from the Good News so that you will be fully prepared. In addition to all of these, hold up the shield of faith to stop the fiery arrows of the devil. Put on salvation as your helmet, and take the sword of the Spirit, which is the word of God. Pray in the Spirit at all times and on every occasion. Stay alert and be persistent in your prayers for all believers everywhere.

- Ephesians 6:10-18 -

Afterwards I felt that I had everything I needed just like the scripture said I had, the *"belt of truth on my waist."* I had the *"breastplate of righteousness on," "my feet were fitted with the readiness that comes from the gospel of peace,"* I had taken up, *"my shield of faith."* I just knew that I was ready to extinguish *"all of the flaming arrows"* that the enemy had been shooting towards my son! I then put on my *"helmet of salvation"* and most importantly, I picked up the *"sword of the Spirit"* which is the word of God! So, with my weapon in hand, I just began to simply pray! I prayed every day for at least an hour for countless days, doing my best to strategically slice through every spiritual stronghold in my son's life:

> *No weapon formed against my son*
> *and I shall prosper, and every tongue*
> *that rises against us in judgment I*
> *condemn. I am established in*
> *righteousness, and oppression is far*
> *from my son and me. The weapons of*

*our warfare are not carnal but
mighty through God to the pulling
down of strongholds. I take the shield
of faith, and I quench every fiery dart
of the enemy. I take the sword of the
Spirit, which is the Word of God,
and use it against the enemy. We are
redeemed from the curse of the law.
We are redeemed from poverty. We
are redeemed from sickness. We are
redeemed from spiritual death. We
overcome all because greater is He
that is us than he that is in the
world. We stand in the evil day
having our loins girded about with
truth, and have the breastplate of*

righteousness. Our feet are shod with the gospel of peace. We take the shield of faith. We are covered with the helmet of salvation, and we use the sword of the Spirit, which is the Word of God. We are delivered from the power of darkness and translated into the kingdom of God's dear Son. We tread upon serpents and scorpions and over all the power of the enemy, and nothing shall hurt me. We do not have the spirit of fear but power, love, and a sound mind. We are blessed with all spiritual blessings in heavenly places in Christ Jesus. We are healed by the

*stripes of Jesus. Our hand is upon
the neck of my enemies. You anoint
our head with oil; our cup runs over.
Goodness and mercy shall follow us
all the days of our lives. We are
anointed to preach, to teach, to heal,
and to cast out devils. We receive an
abundance of grace and the gift of
righteousness, and we reign in life
through Christ Jesus. We have life
and that more abundantly. We walk
in the light as He is in the light, and
the blood of Jesus cleanses us from all
sin. We are the righteousness of God
in Christ. We are the head and not
the tail. We shall decree a thing, and*

*it shall be established in our lives.
We have favor with God and with
man. Wealth and riches are in our
house, and our righteousness
endures forever. We will be satisfied
with long life, and God will show us
His salvation. We dwell in the secret
place of the Most High, and we abide
under the shadow of the Almighty.
No evil will befall us, and no plague
shall come near our dwelling. My
son is taught of the Lord, and great
is his peace. We are strengthened
with might by His Spirit in the inner
man. We are rooted and grounded in
love. We bless my natural enemies,*

and we overcome evil with good.

Lord, bless us and keep us. Make Your face to shine upon us and be gracious unto us. Lord, lift Your countenance upon us and give us peace. Make us as Ephraim and Manasseh. Let us be satisfied with favor and filled with Your blessing. Lord, command Your blessing upon our lives. Give us revelation and let us be blessed. We are the seed of Abraham through Jesus Christ, and we receive the blessing of Abraham. Lord, in blessing, bless us, and in multiplying, multiply us as the stars of heaven and as the sand of the seashore. Let Your showers of blessing be upon our lives. Turn every curse sent our way into a blessing. Let Your blessings make us wealthy. Let all nations call us blessed. Let all generations call us blessed. We are the son/daughter of the blessed. We live in the kingdom of the blessed. Our sins are forgiven, and we are blessed. Lord, You daily load us with benefits. We are chosen by God, and we are blessed. Our seed is blessed. Let us inherit the land. We are a part of a holy nation, and we are blessed. Lord, bless our latter end more than our beginning. Lord, let Your presence bless our lives. We drink the cup of blessing. Lord, bless us and cause Your face to shine upon us, that Your way may be known upon the earth and Your saving health among all nations. Let our

land yield increase, and let the ends of the
earth fear You. I know You favor us because
our enemies do not triumph over us. Lord,
be favorable unto our land. Lord, grant our
lives and favor. In Your favor, Lord, make
our mountain stand strong. Lord, we
entreat Your favor. Let Your favor causes
our horn to be exalted. Lord, this is our set
time for favor. Remember us, O Lord, with
the favor that You bring unto Your children,
and visit us with Your salvation. Lord, we
entreat Your favor with our whole heart. Let
Your favor be upon our lives as a cloud of
the latter rain. Let Your beauty be upon us,
and let us be well-favored. We are highly
favored. Lord, let us receive extraordinary

favor. **Prayers for Revelation:** *You are a God that reveals secrets. Lord, reveal Your secrets unto us. Reveal to us the secret and deep things. Let us understand things kept secret from the foundation of the world. Let the seals be broken from Your Word. Let us understand and have revelation of Your will and purpose for our lives. Give us the spirit of wisdom and revelation, and let the eyes of our understanding be enlightened. Let us understand heavenly things. Open our eyes to behold wondrous things out of Your Word. Let us know and understand the mysteries of the kingdom. Let us speak to others by revelation. Reveal your secrets to Your servants the prophets. Let the hidden* *things be made manifest. Hide Your truths from the wise and prudent, and reveal them to babes. Let Your arm be revealed in our lives. Reveal the things that belong to us. Let Your Word be revealed unto us. Let Your glory be revealed in our lives. Let Your righteousness be revealed in our lives. Let us receive visions and revelations of the Lord. Let us receive an abundance of revelations. Let us be a good steward of Your revelations. Let us speak the mystery of Christ. Let us receive and understand Your hidden wisdom. Hide not Your commandments from us. Let us speak the wisdom of God in a mystery. Let us understand Your parables; the words of the wise and their dark sayings.*

*Lord, lighten our candle and enlighten our
darkness. Make darkness light before us.
Give us the treasures of darkness and hidden
riches in secret places. Let Your candle shine
upon our head. Our spirit is the candle of
the Lord, searching all the inward parts of
our belly. Let us understand the deep things
of God. Let us understand Your deep
thoughts. Let our eyes be enlightened with
Your Word. Our eyes are blessed to see. Let
all spiritual cataracts and scales be removed
from my eyes. Let us comprehend with all
saints what is the breadth and length and
depth and height of Your love. Let your
reins instruct us in the night season and let
us awaken with revelation. We sit in*

*heavenly places in Christ, far above all
principality, power, might, and dominion.
We take our positions in the heavens and
bind the principalities and powers that
operate against our lives in the name of
Jesus. We break and rebuke every program
in the heavens that would operate against
you through the sun, the moon, the stars,
and the constellations. The heavens were
created to be a blessing to our lives. We
receive the rain and blessings from heaven
upon our lives in the name of Jesus. We pray
for angels to be released to war against any
spirit in the heavens assigned to block our
prayers from being answered. We bind the
prince of the power of the air, in the name of*

Jesus. We pray for the floodgates of heaven to be opened over our lives. We pray for an open heaven, and we bind any demonic interference from the heavens in the name of Jesus. Let the evil powers of heaven be shaken in the name of Jesus. Let the heavens drop dew upon Us. Bow the heavens and come down, O Lord. Let the heavens be opened over our lives, and let us see visions. Shake the heavens and fill our houses with Your glory. Let the heavens drop at the presence of God. Show Your wonders in the heavens. Ride upon the heavens and release Your voice, O Lord. Release Your manifold wisdom to the powers in the heavens. Break off of our life any limitations and

restrictions placed on our lives by any evil
spirits in the name of Jesus. I bind and cast
out all python and constrictor spirits in the
name of Jesus. Bless us indeed, and enlarge
our coast. Let Your hand be with us, and
keep us from evil. Cast out our enemies, and
enlarge our borders. Lord, you have
promised to enlarge our borders. Enlarge
our hearts so we can run the way of Your
commandments. Our mouth is enlarged
over our enemies. Enlarge my steps so I can
receive Your wealth and prosperity. I receive
deliverance and enlargement for my life. The
Lord shall increase me more and more, my
children and me. Let Your kingdom and
government increase in my life. Let me

increase in the knowledge of God. O Lord, bless me and increase me. Let me increase exceedingly. Let me increase with the increase of God. Let me increase and abound in love. Increase my greatness, and comfort me on every side. Let me increase in wisdom and stature. Let me increase in strength and confound the adversaries. Let Your grace and favor increase in my life. Let the years of my life be increased. Let the Word of God increase in my life. Bless me in all my increase. Let my giving and tithes increase. Let my latter end greatly increase. Let me grow in grace and in the knowledge of Jesus Christ. I will flourish like a palm tree and grow like cedar in Lebanon. Let my faith *grow exceedingly. The breaker is gone up before me and broken through every limitation and barrier of the enemy. Lord, you are the God of the breakthrough. You have broken forth against my enemies. My branches run over every wall erected by the enemy. I can run through a troop and leap over a wall. Let my line go through all the earth, and my words to the end of the world. I am a joint-heir with Jesus Christ. Give me the heathen for my inheritance and the uttermost part of the earth for my possession.*

Your throne, O Lord, is like a fiery flame. You are the God that answers by fire. A fire goes before You, O Lord, and burns up Your enemies. Lord, release Your fire and burn up the works of darkness. Baptize me with the Holy Ghost and fire. Let Your fire be in my hands to heal the sick and cast out devils. Let Your fire burn in my eyes, my heart, my belly, my mouth, and my feet. Let Your fire be in my tongue to preach and prophesy. I receive tongues of fire. Let Your Word be preached with fire. Make me a minister of fire. Deliver me with Your fire. Let Your fire protect me and cover me. I release the fire of God to burn up the idols of the land. Let the works of witchcraft and occultism be burned in Your fire. Purify my life with Your fire. Let Your fire be released in Zion. Let the spirits of lust and perversion be destroyed

with Your fire. Release the spirit of burning
to burn up the works of darkness. Let Your
flame burns up wicked spirits. Let Your
glory kindles a burning like the burning of a
fire. Cause Your glorious voice to be heard.
Show lightning down Your arm with a
flame of devouring fire, with scattering,
tempest, and hailstones. Let Babylon be as
stubble, and let Your fire burn them. Let
them not be able to deliver themselves from
the power of the flame. Lord, come and
rebuke Your enemies with flames of fire. Let
all flesh see Your fire release. Create upon
Zion a flaming fire by night. Let the fire of
Your presence be released in my life. Let
demons be exposed and cast out with Your

fire. Release Your hot thunderbolts against the enemy. Cast forth lightning, and scatter the enemy. Let Your light be for a fire, and Your Holy One for a flame to burn the briers and thorns in my life.

I release the sword of the Lord against the powers of hell in the name of Jesus. I will whet my glittering sword and render Your vengeance against the enemy. Gird Your sword upon Your thigh, and ride prosperously through the earth. Let your enemies fall by the sword. Let the Assyrian fall with the sword. I release the sword of the Lord against leviathan. Send Your angels with flaming swords to fight my battles in the heavens. I release the two-edged sword to

execute judgments written. Release the
sword out of Your mouth against the enemy.
Releasing the Arrows of the Lord I release
the arrow of the Lord's deliverance in my
life. I release Your sharp arrows into the
heart of the King's enemies. Ordain and
release Your arrows against my persecutors.
Send out Your arrows, and scatter the
enemy. Make my enemies turn their back
with Your arrows upon Your strings. Shoot
out Your arrows, and destroy them. Send
Your arrows abroad. Send out arrows of
light into the kingdom of darkness. Heap
mischief upon them, and spend Your arrows
upon them. Shoot Your arrows upon them,
and let them be wounded suddenly. Let

Your arrow goes forth as lightning against the enemy. Break their bones, and pierce them through with Your arrows. Shoot at Your enemies with Your arrows. Set Your mark upon my enemies for Your arrows. Make Your arrows bright, and release Your vengeance upon my enemies.

I am redeemed from the curse of the law. I break all generational curses of pride, lust, perversion, rebellion, witchcraft, idolatry, poverty, rejection, fear, confusion, addiction, death, and destruction in the name of Jesus. I command all generational spirits that came into my life during conception, in the womb, in the birth canal, and through the umbilical cord to come out in the name of Jesus. I break all spoken curses and negative words that I have spoken over my life in the name of Jesus. I break all spoken curses and negative words spoken over my life by others, including those in authority in the name of Jesus. I command all ancestral spirits of freemasonry, idolatry, witchcraft, false religion, polygamy, lust, and perversion to come out of my life in the name of Jesus. I command all hereditary spirits of lust, rejection, fear, sickness, infirmity, disease, anger, hatred, confusion, failure, and poverty to come out of my life in the name of Jesus. I break the legal rights of all generational spirits operating behind a curse in the name of Jesus. You have no *legal right to operate in my life. I bind and rebuke all familiar spirits and spirit guides that would try to operate in my life from my ancestors in the name of Jesus. I renounce all false beliefs and philosophies inherited by my ancestors in the name of Jesus. I break all curses on my finances from any ancestors that cheated or mishandled money in the name of Jesus. I break all curses of sickness and disease and command all inherited sickness to leave my body in the name of Jesus. Through Jesus, my family is blessed. I renounce all pride inherited from my ancestors in the name of Jesus. I break all oaths, vows, and pacts made with the devil by my ancestors in the name of Jesus. I break* all curses by agents of Satan spoken against my life in secret in the name of Jesus. I break all written curses that would affect my life in the name of Jesus. I break every time-released curse that would activate in my life as I grow older in the name of Jesus. I break every curse Balaam hired against my life in the name of Jesus. Lord, turn every curse spoken against my life into a blessing. I break all generational rebellion that would cause me to resist the Holy Spirit. I break all curses of death spoken by people in authority in my nation over my nation in the name of Jesus. I break curses of death spoken against America by people from other nations in the name of Jesus. Disannulling Ungodly

Covenants, I break and disannul all ungodly covenants, oaths, and pledges I have made with my lips in the name of Jesus. I renounce and break all ungodly oaths made by my ancestors to idols, demons, false religions, or ungodly organizations in the name of Jesus. I break and disannul all covenants with death and hell made by my ancestors in the name of Jesus. I break and disannul all ungodly covenants made with idols or demons by my ancestors in the name of Jesus. I break and disannul all blood covenants made through sacrifice that would affect my life in the name of Jesus. I command all demons that claim any legal right to my life through covenants to come

out in the name of Jesus. I break and
disannul any covenant made with false gods
and demons through the occult involvement
and witchcraft in the name of Jesus. I break
and disannul all spirit marriages that would
cause incubus and succubus demons to
attack my life in the name of Jesus. I break
and disannul any marriage to any demon
that would affect my life in the name of
Jesus. I break all agreements with hell in the
name of Jesus. I have a covenant with God
through the blood of Jesus Christ. I am
joined to the Lord, and I am one spirit with
Him. I break all ungodly covenants and
renew my covenant to God through the body
and blood of Jesus. I divorce myself from any

*demon that would claim my life through any
ancestral covenants in the name of Jesus. I
bind and cast out any family demon that
would follow my life through ancestral
covenants in the name of Jesus.*

*I cover myself, my family, and my
possessions with the blood of Jesus. Let the
fire of God surround and protect my life
from all destruction. Let the angel of the
Lord encamp around me and protect me. Let
Your glory be my covering and protect my
back. Hold me up, and I will be safe. The
name of Jesus is a strong tower. I run into
it, and I am safe. Lord, you make me to dwell
in safety. Set me in safety from them who
puff at me. Let me dwell in my land safely*

Lead me safely, and I will not fear. Let the sea overwhelm my enemies. Let me lie down and rest in safety. I will dwell in safety; nothing shall make me afraid. Keep me as the apple of Your eye, and hide me under the shadow of Your wings. I will trust in the cover of Your wings. In the shadow of Your wings will I trust. Be my covert from the storm and the rain. Be my covert from the wind and the tempest. Cover my head in the day of battle. Cover me with the shadow of Your hand. Cover me with Your feathers. Be my defense and refuge. Defend and deliver me. Let Your glory be my defense. Defend me from those who rise up against me. Lord, you are my shield and my hiding place.

Lord, surround me with Your shield of protection. Bring them down, O Lord, my shield. Let Your truth be my shield. Lord, you are my sun and shield. Lord, you are my shield and exceeding great reward. I will not be afraid of ten thousand that have set themselves against me, because You are a shield for me. You are a strong tower from the enemy. Prayers to Release the Arm of the Lord No one has an arm like You, Lord, full of power and might. Lord, you have a mighty arm. Your hand is strong, and Your right hand is high. Stretch out Your arm and deliver me, and rid me out of all bondage. Let fear and dread fall upon the enemy by the greatness of Your arm until I

pass over. Favor me, and let Your right arm
bring me into my possession. Break Rahab
in pieces, and scatter Your enemies with
Your strong arm. Let Your hand establishes
me, and let Your arm strengthen me. Your
right hand and Your holy arm give me
victory. Show lightning down Your arm
against my enemies. I trust in Your arm for
my salvation. Awake, awake, and put on
strength, O arm of the Lord. Awake as in the
ancient days. Cut Rahab, and wound the
dragon. Make bare Your holy arm in the
sight of all nations, and let all flesh see Your
salvation. Show strength with Your arm,
and scatter the proud. Reveal Your arm
unto me, that I might know Your strength

and power. Let the power in Your hands be released in my life. Releasing the Power of God Lord, release Your glorious power against the enemy. Let power and might be released from Your hand. Scatter the enemy by Your power. Rule over Your enemies through Your power. Let the power of Your anger be released against the powers of darkness. I release the power and authority of the Lord against all demons I encounter in the name of Jesus. I am delivered from the power of Satan unto God. Divide the sea, and destroy marine spirits through Your power. I am strong in the Lord and in the power of His might. Cause the powers of darkness to submit to Your power. Display

Your awesome power that men will believe.
Release Your power in healing and
deliverance. Release Your powerful voice.
Let me be amazed at Your power. Let great
power be released through Your apostles. Let
signs, wonders, and miracles be released
through the power of the Holy Spirit. Let me
preach and teach with demonstration of the
Spirit and power. Let Your power work in
me. Release Your powerful angels on my
behalf to fight my battles in the heavens.
Release the power of Elijah through Your
prophets. Let me be willing in the day of
Your power. Releasing the Power of the
Blood I cover my mind and thoughts with
the blood of Jesus. I cover my doorpost and

possessions with the blood of Jesus. I
overcome the devil through the blood of
Jesus. I sprinkle the blood of Jesus and
receive multiplied grace and peace. I am
made perfect through the blood of the
everlasting covenant. I have boldness to
enter into the presence of God through the
blood. My conscience is purged from dead
works to serve the living God through the
blood of Jesus. I eat the body of Jesus and
drink His blood. I have redemption through
the blood of Jesus, and I am redeemed from
the power of evil. I rebuke all spirits of
torment and fear because I have peace
through the blood of Jesus. I receive the
benefits of the new covenant through the

blood of Jesus. I receive healing and health through the blood of Jesus. I receive abundance and prosperity through the blood of Jesus. I receive deliverance through the blood of Jesus. I receive the fullness of the Holy Spirit and the anointing through the blood of Jesus. The blood of Jesus bears witness to my deliverance and salvation. The blood of Jesus cleanses me from all sin. Jesus resisted unto blood, and His blood gives me victory. I rebuke and cast out all spirits of guilt, shame, and condemnation through the blood of Jesus. I break the power of sin and iniquity in my life through the blood of Jesus. My heart is sprinkled and purified by the blood of Jesus from an evil conscience. I rebuke Satan, the accuser of the brethren, through the blood of Jesus. I command all my accusers to depart through the blood of Jesus. I rebuke and cast out all spirits of slander and accusation through the blood of Jesus. I release the voice of the blood against demons and evil spirits that would accuse and condemn me.

Warfare Prayers: *Lord, teach my hands to war and my fingers to fight. Lord, I am Your End-Times Warrior. Use me as Your weapon against the enemy. The weapons of my warfare are not carnal, but mighty through You to the pulling down of strongholds. Satan, you have lost the war in heaven. Let all the enemies that make war*

with the Lamb be destroyed. I do not war
after the flesh but after the spirit. Lord,
thunder upon the enemy; release Your voice;
hail stones and coals of fire. Send out Your
arrows, and scatter them. Shoot out Your
light and discomfit them. Deliver me from
my strong enemy, from them that are too
strong for me. Deliver me, and bring me
into a large place. I am your battle-ax and
weapon of war. You have given me the necks
of my enemies, and I will destroy them in
the name of Jesus. I am Your anointed, and
You give me great deliverance. I will beat
them small as the dust and cast them out as
mire in the streets. I have pursued my
enemies and overtaken them. I did not turn

until they were consumed. I have wounded them, and they are not able to rise. They have fallen under my feet I tread upon the lion and adder. The young lion and dragon I trample underfoot. I tread upon serpents and scorpions and over all the power of the enemy, and nothing shall by any means hurt me. I tread down the wicked; they are ashes under my feet. I will arise and thresh and beat the enemy into pieces. I rebuke every wild boar of the field in the name of Jesus. I rebuke every spirit that creeps forth from the forest. I rebuke every beast of the forest that comes to devour. I rebuke every lion of the forest that comes to slay. I close the door to every demonic rat that would attempt to

come into my life in the name of Jesus. I
bind and cast out every thief that would try
to steal my finances in the name of Jesus. I
bind and cast out any spirit that would try
to steal my joy in the name of Jesus. I bind,
expose, and cast out any demon that would
try by stealth (undetected) to come into my
life. Lord, cleanse my temple and drive out
any thief from my life. Lord, lift up a
standard against any flood the enemy would
try to bring into my life. I bind and cast out
all familiar spirits that would try to operate
in my life in the name of Jesus. I bind and
rebuke any demon that would try to block
my way in the name of Jesus. I remove all
leaven of malice and wickedness from my

life. I rebuke and cast out any froglike spirit from my life in the name of Jesus. I bind and rebuke devils in high places in the name of Jesus. I break off any fellowship with devils through sin, the flesh, or sacrifice in the name of Jesus. I command all devils to leave my children in the name of Jesus. Lord, expose any human devils in my life in the name of Jesus. Lord, expose any children of the devil that would try to come into the church. Let every spirit hiding from me be exposed in the name of Jesus. Let every hidden snare for my feet be exposed. I stand against and rebuke every wile of the devil. I release myself from any snare of the devil in the name of Jesus. I will not come into the

condemnation of the devil. Lord, let no
doctrine of the devil be established in my life.
I nullify the power of any sacrifice made to
devils in my city, region, or nation in the
name of Jesus. I bind and rebuke Molech and
any spirit that has been assigned to abort my
destiny. Give me strength to bring forth my
destiny. I overcome every antichrist spirit
because greater is He that is in me than he
that is in the world. I lose myself from every
spirit of error in the name of Jesus. Lord, let
me not operate in the wrong spirit. I lose
myself from every spirit of whoredom in the
name of Jesus. Let me have and walk in an
excellent spirit. I will take heed to my spirit
at all times. I bind and cast out any spirit

that would try to tear apart my life in any manner in the name of Jesus. Lord, stir up my spirit to do Your will. I bind and cast out any demon of slumber from my life in the name of Jesus. I bind and cast out all demons of fear and timidity in the name of Jesus. I bind and cast out all seducing spirits that would come my way in the name of Jesus. I bind and rebuke the angel of light in the name of Jesus. I reject all false apostolic ministries in the name of Jesus. I reject all false prophetic ministries in the name of Jesus. I reject all false teaching ministries in the name of Jesus. Expose all false brethren to me. I reject the mouth of vanity and the right hand of falsehood. I reject every false

vision and every false prophetic word
released into my life. I bind Satan, the
deceiver, from releasing any deception into
my life. I bind and cast out all spirits of self-
deception in the name of Jesus. I bind and
cast out any spirit of sorcery that would
deceive me in the name of Jesus. Lord, let no
man deceive me. I bind and rebuke any
bewitchment that would keep me from
obeying the truth. I pray for utterance and
boldness to make known the mystery of the
gospel. Deliver me out of the hand of wicked
and unreasonable men. Evil spirits leave my
life as I hear and speak the Word. I rebuke,
still, and cast out the avenger. I bind and
cast out any creeping spirit that would

attempt to creep into my life. Let the hammer of the wicked be broken. I renounce all earthly, sensual, and demonic wisdom. I cast out devils, and I will be perfected. Let every Pharaoh that would pursue my life be drowned in the sea. I rebuke every demonic bee that would surround me in the name of Jesus. I bind and cast out any spirit of Absalom that would try to steal my heart from God's ordained leadership. I will sleep well. I will not be kept awake by any spirit of restlessness or insomnia. I laugh at the enemy through the Holy Spirit. I cut the cords of the wicked from my life. Let every cord the enemy tries to put around my life be like burning flax. I break down every wall of Jericho. Lord, cleanse my life from secret faults. Lord, let Your secret be upon my tabernacle. Lead me and guide me for Your name's sake. Guide me continually. Guide me into all truth. Guide me with Your eye. Let me guide my affairs with discretion. Guide me by the skillfulness of Your hands. Lead me in a plain path because of my enemies. Lead me not into temptation, but deliver me from evil. Lead me, and make Your way straight before my eyes. Make the crooked places straight and the rough places smooth before me. Send out Your light and truth, and let them lead me. Make darkness light before me and crooked things straight. Teach me to do your will, and lead me into the land of uprightness. I put on the garment of praise for the spirit of heaviness. Clothe me with the garment of salvation. I put on my beautiful garment. Let my garments always be white. Let me be clothed with humility. Cover me with the robe of righteousness. Let my clothes be full of Your virtue. Let a mantle of power rest upon my life. Lord, give me wisdom in every area where I lack.

Prayers to Rout Out Demons: *Let every plant that my Father has not planted be rooted out in the name of Jesus. I lay the ax to the root of every evil tree in my life. Let every ungodly generational taproot be cut and pulled out of my bloodline in the name*

*of Jesus. Let the roots of wickedness be as
rottenness. I speak to every evil tree to be
uprooted and cast into the sea. Let Your holy
fire burns up every ungodly root in the
name of Jesus. Let the confidence of the
enemy be rooted out. Let every root of
bitterness be cut from my life. Let the
prophetic word be released to root out evil
kingdoms. Let any evil person planted in my
church be rooted out in the name of Jesus.
Let any sickness rooted in my body be
plucked up in the name of Jesus. Let all false
ministries that have rooted themselves in my
city be plucked up. Let every bramble and
nettle be plucked up from my life in the
name of Jesus. Let all thorns be burned out*

of my life in the name of Jesus. Let all spirits rooted in rejection come out in the name of Jesus. Let all spirits rooted in pride come out in the name of Jesus. Let all spirits rooted in rebellion come out in the name of Jesus. Let all spirits rooted in fear come out in the name of Jesus. Let all spirits rooted in lust and sexual sin come out in the name of Jesus. Let all spirits rooted in curses come out in the name of Jesus. Let all spirits rooted in witchcraft come out in the name of Jesus. Let all spirits rooted in any part of my body and organs come out in the name of Jesus.

Prayers Against Satan (the Devil):

Satan, *I rebuke thee. Get thee hence, Satan,*

for it is written. Get behind me, Satan, for it is written. I beheld Satan as lightning fall from heaven. I loose myself from every bond of Satan in the name of Jesus. Lord, bruise Satan under my feet. I bind and rebuke all hindering spirits of Satan in the name of Jesus. I renounce all ungodly anger, and I give no place to the devil. I pray to overcome any sifting that Satan would try to bring into my life. I am delivered from the power of Satan unto God. I bind the thief from stealing, killing, or destroying in my life. Lord, remove Satan's seat from my region, city, and nation. Lord, remove every synagogue of Satan from my city, region, and nation. I bind and rebuke all wrath of the devil directed against my life. Devil, I resist you. Flee! I am sober and vigilant against my adversary, the devil. Rebuking the Enemy Satan, the Lord rebukes thee. Let the enemy perish at Your rebuke, O Lord. Let the enemy flee at Your rebuke, O Lord. I rebuke all the winds and storms of the enemy sent against my life. Rebuke the company of the spearmen and the multitude of the bulls until they submit. Rebuke those that rush at me, and let them flee away. Rebuke the devourer for my sake. Rebuke the horse and chariot, and let them fall into a deep sleep. I rebuke every unclean spirit that would attempt to operate in my life. I rebuke the proud spirits that are cursed. I release furious rebukes upon the enemy. Let the blast of your nostrils rebuke the enemy. Rebuke the enemy with flames of fire. Let a thousand flee at my rebuke, O Lord. Rebuke every sea that would try to close upon my life. Devil, I rebuke you. Hold your peace, and come out.

Speaking to Mountains: *I speak to every mountain in my life and command it to be removed and cast into the sea. I speak to every financial mountain to be removed from my life in the name of Jesus. Let every evil mountain hear the voice of the Lord and be removed. I prophesy to the mountains and command them to hear the Word of the Lord and be removed. Let the mountains* tremble at the presence of God. I contend with every mountain and command them to hear my voice. Lay the mountain of Esau (the flesh) to waste. Put forth Your hand, O Lord, and overturn the mountains by the roots. I speak to every mountain of debt to be removed and cast into the sea. Lord, you are against every destroying mountain. Let the mountains melt at Your presence, O God. Make waste the evil mountains in my life, O Lord I thresh every mountain, I beat them small, and I make the hills as chaff. Every mountain in my way will become a plain.

Releasing the Spoilers: *Let the counsel of the wicked be spoiled. Lead the princes of darkness away spoiled. Let the stouthearted* be spoiled. I bind the enemy, strip him of his armor, and divide his spoils. I release the spoilers to come upon Babylon and destroy her. I release the spoilers to come upon the high places in the name of Jesus. Lord, you have spoiled principalities and powers. I spoil the enemy and take back his goods, in the name of Jesus. I spoil the tents of the enemy in the name of Jesus. I spoil those that have attempted to spoil me. The enemy will not spoil me, but he will be spoiled. Let the palaces and headquarters of darkness be spoiled in the name of Jesus. Let the proud spirits be spoiled in the name of Jesus. I release the cankerworm to spoil the works of darkness in the name of Jesus. Let the *fortresses of darkness be spoiled in the name of Jesus.*

Lord, you created the high places for Your glory. Let not the enemy control the high places. I bind the prince of the power of the air. I bind the powers of darkness that would control the airwaves and release filth, violence, and witchcraft through the media in the name of Jesus. I take authority over the princes of media in the name of Jesus. I bind spiritual wickedness in high places. Lord, destroy the idols in high places. I pluck down the high places of the enemy. I am a king, and I break down the high places in the name of Jesus. I remove Nehushtan (previous moves of God that have become

idols) from the high places. I remove the
religious spirits from the high places. Let the
high place of Tophet be removed. Let Your
holy fire burn up the high places. Let the
high places of witchcraft be destroyed in the
name of Jesus. Destroy all false worship in
the high places. Let the high places be
purged through Your anointing. Remove
every false ministry in high places. Remove
all strange gods from the high places.
Remove every satanic altar erected in the
high places. Let all high places established by
any ungodly ruler be removed in the name
of Jesus. Let all the high places of Baal be
broken down. I prophesy to the ancient high
places and dispossess the enemy. Let

righteous men with Your wisdom sit in the high governmental places of my city and nation. I will walk upon the high places. Let every high place of wickedness that has not been removed be removed. Let me ride upon the high places of the earth, and let me eat the increase of the fields, and let me suck honey out of the rock and oil out of the flinty rock. Let all high places built by my ancestors be removed. Let not the high places our spiritual fathers destroyed to be rebuilt. Let the high places be desolate. I tread upon the high places of the wicked. I break the power of any sacrifice done in the high places. I walk in the spirit of Josiah to deal with the high places. Lord, open rivers in high places. Through Jesus let me possess the gate of the enemy. Establish the gates of praise in my life. I release battering rams against the gates of hell. The gates of hell cannot prevail against me. Let the gates of my life and city be open to the King of glory. Open to me the gates of righteousness that I may enter in. Strengthen the bars of my gates. Break the gates of brass, and cut in sunder the bars of iron. Open before me the gates, that I may go in and receive the treasure of darkness and hidden riches of secret places. I rebuke every enemy in the gates. Let all the gates of my life and city be repaired through the Holy Spirit. Let the valley gate be repaired. Let the gate of the *fountain (represents the flow of the Holy Spirit) be repaired. Let the sheep gate (represents the apostolic) be repaired. Let the fish gate (represents evangelism) be repaired. Let the old gate (represents moves of the past) be repaired. Let the dung gate (represents deliverance) be repaired. Let the water gate (represents preaching and teaching) be repaired. Let the east gate (represents the glory) be repaired. Let the waters flow through the utter gate into my life, past my ankles, past my loins, and past my neck. Make my gates of carbuncles. My gates will be open continually to receive blessings. I command the north gate, the south gate, the east gate, and the west gate*

to open in my city to the King of glory. I
rebuke all enemies that would stand at the
gates and try to stop salvation from entering
in. I pray for the apostolic gatekeepers of my
city to arise and take their place. Let the
gates of my life and city be shut to
uncleanness, witchcraft, drugs, perversion,
and wickedness in the name of Jesus. I pray
for the gateway cities in my nation to
become gateways of righteousness and not
iniquity. Lord, raise up bethel churches that
will be the gate of heaven. Lord, raise up
apostolic gate churches that will usher
presence and revelation into my region.
Prayers Against Idols: *Let any idol in my
life or nation be destroyed and burned with*

Your fire. Lord, cut down all the idols in the land. Let the familiar spirits, wizards, and idols be taken out of the land. Let the idols be confounded and the images be broken into pieces. Let men throw away their idols and turn to You, O Lord. I renounce all idolatry in my bloodline and break all curses of idolatry in the name of Jesus. Lord, put the names of the idols out of the land. I will keep myself from idols. Abolish the idols in America and the nations. Lord, expose all idols as lying vanities. I renounce all covetousness; I will not serve the god of mammon. Let Babylon, the mother of harlots and abominations of the earth, fall in the name of Jesus. Lord, cleanse the pollution of

idols from the land. Sprinkle clean water
upon me, and cleanse me from all filthiness,
and cleanse me from all idols. Let me not go
astray after any idol. Let all false gods and
idols (including humans) be removed from
my life in the name of Jesus. I will put no
other gods before You, Lord.

Prayers That Destroy Oppression: I
rebuke and cast out any spirit that would
attempt to oppress me in the name of Jesus.
Jesus, you went about doing good and
healing all those oppressed of the devil. I
strip all power from spirits that would
oppress me. I rebuke and cast out all spirits
of poverty that would oppress me. I rebuke
all spirits of madness and confusion that

would attempt to oppress my mind in the name of Jesus. O Lord, undertake for me against all my oppressors. Lord, you are my refuge from the oppressor. Deliver me from the wicked that would oppress me and from my deadly enemies that would surround me. Deliver me from oppressors that seek after my soul. Break-in pieces the oppressor. I rebuke and cast out all spirits of affliction, sorrow, and anything attempting to bring me low in the name of Jesus. Leave me not to my oppressors. Let not the proud oppress me. Deliver me from the oppression of men. I rule over my oppressors. Let the oppressors be consumed out of the land. I rebuke the voice of the oppressor in the name of Jesus. I

am established in righteousness, and I am
far from oppression. Punish those who
attempt to oppress me. Th e enemy will not
take my inheritance through oppression.
Execute judgment against my oppressors.

**Breaking the Power of Schizophrenia
and Doublemindedness:** *I bind and
rebuke every spirit that would attempt to
distort, disturb, or disintegrate the
development of my personality in the name
of Jesus. I bind and break all curses of
schizophrenia and doublemindedness on my
family, in the name of Jesus. I bind and
rebuke the spirit of doublemindedness in the
name of Jesus. I bind and take authority over
the strongmen of rejection and rebellion and*

separate them in the name of Jesus. I bind
and cast out the spirits of rejection, fear of
rejection, and self-rejection in the name of
Jesus. I bind and cast out all spirits of lust,
fantasy lust, harlotry, and perverseness in
the name of Jesus. I bind and cast out all
spirits of insecurity and inferiority in the
name of Jesus. I bind and cast out all spirits
of self-accusation and compulsive confession
in the name of Jesus. I bind and cast out all
spirits of fear of judgment, self-pity, false
compassion, and false responsibility in the
name of Jesus. I bind and cast out all spirits
of depression, despondency, despair,
discouragement, and hopelessness in the
name of Jesus. I bind and cast out all spirits

of guilt, condemnation, unworthiness, and shame in the name of Jesus. I bind and cast out all spirits of perfection, pride, vanity, ego, intolerance, frustration, and impatience in the name of Jesus. I bind and cast out all spirits of unfairness, withdrawal, pouting, unreality, fantasy, daydreaming, and vivid imagination in the name of Jesus. I bind and cast out all spirits of self-awareness, timidity, loneliness, and sensitivity in the name of Jesus. I bind and cast out all spirits of talkativeness, nervousness, tension, and fear in the name of Jesus. I bind and cast out all spirits of self-will, selfishness, and stubbornness in the name of Jesus. I bind and cast out the spirit of accusation in the *name of Jesus. I bind and cast out all spirits of self-delusion, self-deception, and self-seduction in the name of Jesus. I bind and cast out all spirits of judgment, pride, and un-teachable-ness in the name of Jesus. I bind and cast out all spirits of control and possessiveness in the name of Jesus. I bind and cast out the root of bitterness in the name of Jesus. I bind and cast out all spirits of hatred, resentment, violence, murder, unforgiveness, anger, and retaliation in the name of Jesus. I bind and cast out spirits of paranoia, suspicion, distrust, persecution, confrontation, and fear in the name of Jesus.*

Prayers and Decrees That Break the Powers of Darkness: *Let the Assyrian be* broken in my land. Break-in pieces the gates of brass and cut the bars of iron. I break every yoke from off my neck, and I burst all the bonds in the name of Jesus. Break them with the rod of iron, and dash them in pieces like a potter's vessel. Break the arm of the wicked. Break their teeth, O God, in their mouths. Break the teeth of the young lions. Let the oppressor be broken into pieces. Let the arms of the wicked be broken. Let the horns of the wicked be broken. Let the kingdoms of darkness be broken. Let the foundations of the wicked be broken. Let the kingdoms of Babylon be broken. Let all the bows of the wicked be broken. I break into pieces the horse and the rider. I break into pieces the chariot and the rider. I break in pieces the captains and the rulers. Let Your Word out of my mouth be like a hammer that breaks the rocks into pieces. Break down every wall erected by the enemy against my life. I break down every altar erected by the enemy against my life in the name of Jesus. Let the idols and images of the land be broken by Your power, O Lord. I break and disannul every demonic covenant made by my ancestors in the name of Jesus. I bind and cast out the spirit of Apollyon (Abaddon) in the name of Jesus. I am redeemed from destruction. I break all curses of destruction in my family and bloodline in the name of Jesus. I renounce all pride that *would open the door for destruction. Rescue my soul from destructions. Send Your Word, and deliver me from any destruction. The destroyer cannot come into my life or family in the name of Jesus. The destroyer cannot destroy my prosperity. I am delivered from the destruction that wastes at noonday. There is no wasting or destruction within my borders. I will enter in at the straight gate, and I will not walk in the path that leads to destruction. I bind the spirit of mammon that leads to destruction. I will keep my mouth and avoid destruction. I bind and rebuke the spirit of poverty that leads to destruction. I rebuke all destruction from my gates in the name of Jesus.*

Closing Breaches and Hedges: *I close up any breach in my life that would give Satan and demons access in the name of Jesus. I pray for every broken hedge in my life to be restored in the name of Jesus. I stand in the gap and make up the hedge. I repent and receive forgiveness for any sin that has opened the door for any spirit to enter and operate in my life. I am a rebuilder of the wall and a repairer of the breach. I renounce all crooked speech that would cause a breach in the name of Jesus. Bind up all my breaches, O Lord. Let every breach be stopped in the name of Jesus. Let my walls be salvation and my gates praise. I pray for a hedge of protection around my mind, body,* *finances, possessions, and family in the name of Jesus.* **Destroying Evil Cauldrons (Pots)***: I rebuke and destroy every wicked cauldron in the name of Jesus. I rebuke and destroy every seething pot or cauldron stirred up by the enemy against my life, city, or nation. Let every wicked cauldron in my city be broken in the name of Jesus. I break every witchcraft cauldron stirred up by witches and warlocks in the name of Jesus. Lord, visit every witch and warlock in my region and convict. Let them repent, turn to You, and be saved. I am delivered from the boiling pot in the name of Jesus. Lord, bring me out of the midst of every cauldron. The enemy will not eat my* *flesh, break my bones, and put me in his cauldron. Lord, deliver and protect me from every pot of evil in the name of Jesus. Lord, deliver me from the boiling pot of pride.*

Destroying Yokes and Removing Burdens: *I remove all false burdens placed on me by people, leaders, or churches in the name of Jesus. I remove all heavy burdens placed on my life by the enemy in the name of Jesus. Let your anointing break the enemy's burden from off my neck, and let every yoke be destroyed. Remove my shoulder from every burden. I cast my cares upon the Lord. I cast my burdens upon the Lord, and He sustains me. Lord, break the yoke of the enemy's burden and break the* *staff and the rod of the oppressor as in the day of Midian. Let every yoke of poverty be destroyed in the name of Jesus. Let every yoke of sickness be destroyed in the name of Jesus. Let every yoke of bondage be destroyed in the name of Jesus. Let every unequal yoke be broken in the name of Jesus. I destroy every yoke and burden of religion and legalism on my life by religious leaders in the name of Jesus. Let every burdensome stone be released from my life in the name of Jesus. I take upon my life the yoke and burden of Jesus. I uproot, bind, and cast out the spirit of fear, anger, drugs, smoking, rejection, drinking, murder, suicide, temper, bitterness, hatred, pornography, witchcraft, disobedience, perversion, rebellion, unforgiveness, brokenness, depression, anxiety, hurt, pride, lust, sadness, self-pity, shame, torment, envy, self-rejections, stress, self-unforgiveness, inadequacy, sorrow, self-doubt, broken heartedness, guilt, paranoia, rage, hostility, strife, implacable, disobedience, boastful, slander, gossip, deceit, insolence, maliciousness, fornication, unrighteousness, bondage, and doublemindedness. I render it powerless in the name of Jesus, I decree and declare this over my sin in the name of Jesus!*

!!! I PRAYED E.V.E.R.Y. DAY !!!

2

MY JOB EXPERIENCE
(Kakopatheo)

Things seem to be going better by

this point. I was blessed with a new

home and my son was home. I even got

a prophetic word around March of 2020

and the word was, Zanetta De'Vyon is

going to be ok. I held onto that word for

dear life. As the months progressed, I

was able to stop stressing so much and

began to trust God to take care of my

most precious gift. Afterall, in church it is said that *faith is letting go and allowing God to be God.*

De'Vyon decided to go ahead and attend college after receiving a football scholarship from Arkansas Baptist College. I paid his dorm deposit and was waiting to get the room assignment. In the interim, his cousin helped him get a job and this job actually could've ended up being a career. He ran into a hiccup though. The day he was to start training, the

company issued a temporary hiring

freeze. I will never forget the day. It was

June 17, 2020. It started out as an

ordinary day. I woke up and started my

day as usual with a few appointments

on my schedule. On the other hand,

De'Vyon's day was typical and normal

for him. He had graduated the month

prior and he just wanted to "let his hair

down and live a little" as he put it! He

just wanted to paint the town red before

leaving for college. Little did I know, it would be his blood that did just that! At about around 6:30 pm my phone begins to ring! One of his best friends his brother as he always called him Daylyn calls, "Ma, where's De'Vyon?" I responded, "I don't know baby?" Daylyn responded with panic in his voice, "you need to call him and find out where he is!" Before I could even make the call, I got another call. This time, it was my son's old coach,

"Zanetta, where's De'Vyon?" I

responded once again with my heart

pounding, "I don't know, I am trying to

contact him now!" Immediately, he says,

"Zanetta, you need to get to Merritt

Island!" I said to the coach, "what's

going on?" All he would say was,

"Zanetta, you need to get here!" So, I

jumped up and headed to Merritt

Island. As I began to head to Merritt

Island, my phone began blowing up

with text messages... *Zanetta, are you ok?*

Zanetta, I'm sorry for your loss! I get to

Merritt Island to the apartment complex

and get out of the car and the apartment

complex is roped off and I come face to

face with a police officer! My first

question to him, "where's my son?" He

commences to tell me that my son was

not there and that he was rushed to the

hospital so I left and went to the

hospital! I get to the hospital and no one

is giving me any information! So, I'm

pacing back and forth and also trying to

contact my family, my Apostle and close family friends! After what felt like forever, the hospital staff came and took me into a small white room that had chairs, one big window and a small table; that's it nothing, nothing less. While I was in that room, I instantly fell to my knees and began to worship and pray! I did not care who could see me or hear me, I just prayed! Tears rolled down my face like continuous water cascading from a waterfall. Time had no value because I am not sure   how

long after they placed me in that room

that two police officers finally showed

up and began questioning my mother

and me about identifying marks on my

son's body. It was as if they were

stalling with what they had to tell me. In

my mind, I kept thinking that this is

going to be his wake-up call! He would

finally get it together after this close call.

This was not to be the case though.

Instead, the words they spoke was like

an earthquake shaking the ground

beneath my feet… "Ma'am, I am sorry,

but your son is dead! Dead? In my

mind, I was thinking, what do you

mean dead? My mother and I both

collapsed to the floor screaming! I do

not know how long we were on that

floor in despair because everything was

a blur. At some point, I got up and

walked out of the hospital and I just

began to walk! I didn't know where I

was going, but I was propelled forward

to an unknown destination. Some family members including my Apostle, my Pastor, my cousin, and my son's girlfriend followed behind me and I am certain there was a trail of tears. I walked and they remained in tow with every step that I took to nowhere. Then it was as if God arrested me and I stopped and released this massive explosive, glass shattering scream that literally sent a shockwaves of pain down my spinal cord like a mother in

labor fighting the pain of contractions.
My knees couldn't hold the weight of
the internal anguish inside of me and I
literally collapsed. As I crumpled to my
knees on that dark, gritty asphalt
Apostle Shauna and Pastor Latice tried
to break my fall and catch me. I
remember the texture and coolness of
the asphalt connecting with my face as
my tears rolled down my face
incessantly, landing on the ground. The
concrete was so cold like the one that

had no regard for snatching the life of my son. The agonizing pain ending in silent screams from the depths of my shattered soul.

At some point, my Apostle's husband picked me up off the ground like a father helping their daughter up from falling off a bike with care and compassion. He sat me in the trunk of their truck which allowed me to try and gain my composure. Once again, a cop tried to talk to me. His lips were moving, but I heard nothing. I just wanted to see my son, but they would not let me! All I remember is trying to push through him and anyone else that was holding me back, I just didn't care! Eventually, I got weak again and my Apostle's husband walked me back to the hospital's emergency room and sat me in a chair and again the police tried to talk to me, but again their words fell on deaf ears!

As I sat in that chair, it was like my soul as well as my spirit left my body. I was just a shell sitting there like a zombie with all of the tears and pain suffocating all my emotions, just GONE! Everyone that knows me can attest to how important my son was to me! I love expensive and extravagant things, but God could have taken all of my possessions, my car, my money, my home, but instead my son was taken from me! I would've lived in a hut or under a bridge as long as I knew my

boy was going to be ok! But for

whatever reason God allowed my entire

world to be destroyed in an instant!

That instant was confirmed with,

"Ma'am I'm sorry but your son is dead!"

And now I was at a crossroad…I

was either going to revert back to a

lifestyle I had long abandoned and kill

everyone involved or I was going to be

who God says that I am. So, in my

sleepwalker state, I stood in the middle

of that crossroad, which was in the

middle of my hollow heart, and made

my choice…

"This command I am giving you
today is not too difficult for you, and it is
not beyond your reach. It is not kept in
heaven, so distant that you must ask, 'Who
will go up to heaven and bring it down so
we can hear it and obey? It is not kept
beyond the sea, so far away that you must
ask, 'Who will cross the sea to bring it to us
so we can hear it and obey?' No, the message
is very close at hand; it is on your lips and
in your heart so that you can obey it. "Now
listen! Today, I am giving you a choice
between life and death, between prosperity
and disaster. For I command you this day to
love the LORD your God and to keep his
commands, decrees, and regulations by
walking in his ways. If you do this, you will
live and multiply, and the LORD your God

will bless you and the land you are about to
enter and occupy. "But if your heart turns
away and you refuse to listen, and if you are
drawn away to serve and worship other
gods, [18] then I warn you now that you will
certainly be destroyed. You will not live a
long, good life in the land you are crossing
the Jordan to occupy.

"Today I have given you the choice
between life and death, between blessings
and curses. Now I call on heaven and earth
to witness the choice you make. Oh, that you
would choose life so that you and your
descendants might live! [20] You can make this
choice by loving the LORD your God,
obeying him, and committing yourself
firmly to him. This is the key to your life.
And if you love and obey the LORD, you will
live long in the land the LORD swore to give
your ancestors Abraham, Isaac, and Jacob."
                              - Deuteronomy 30:15-16

I looked at everyone around me and with a splintered heart, I chose to continue following Christ! Sitting there in that zombie like state, feeling nothing but heartache, God filled my empty shell and in that very moment, it was GOD OVER EVERYTHING!

3

MY YES
(Zugos)

Now anyone who knew the old

Zanetta...the B.C., *(before Christ)* version

of Zanetta knew my capabilities. They

knew what my family could do as well!

However, even in my darkest

hour, I still found the strength to say,

"yes," I lay aside my will for your will, God!

I will serve you and obey! Truthfully,

my yes in that moment blew my own

mind! Why? In my family, we were raised to take care of our family at any means necessary. Honestly, the ones who had taken my son's life would have been dead too.

However, when God said,

"Zanetta you have been my servant for 11 years. You have too much in you to throw it all away! I need you to trust me and obey! I need your yes!"

You are to distinguish between the holy and the common, and between the unclean and the clean,

- Leviticus 10:10- (ESV)

Somehow, I found the strength to continue to follow God and my choice gave me peace. I was able to find supernatural strength to just trust Him and obey! I know that I did that because I knew that if I acted on all the devastation and rage, it would only lead to more bloodshed, more mothers crying and more young people dying. The A.D. (*after Christ*) version of me would not and could not allow that to

happen! I did not want my family or

anyone else to have their lives shattered

by another senseless death!! I refused to

be a instrument the enemy used destroy

my family further. Instead, I desired to

pick up the shattered pieces and be

medicine for someone else's wounds so

I surrendered and followed the

Shepherd's lead.

4

MY HARD PLACE

(Poros)

Despite surrendering to God, I began to struggle with old emotions and new demons! In my previous works, I shared that one of my biggest strongholds was homosexuality. When my son was murdered, it was like all my old girlfriends started contacting me! Before I continue let me make this clear, I have been delivered from the homosexuality stronghold, However, just because deliverance has taken place, doesn't mean enemy stops dangling bait! It is up to the individual to say yes or no because we all have free will to choose!

So now that, that is out of the way, like I said, "I had to face several of my ex-girlfriends when my son died!" Now there was one, let us just call her Jade that I dated before I entered the military. Our relationship was tumultuous oftentimes. Jade had never been with a woman before me, and I guess the situation was an emotional roller coaster. Afterall, there was no play book for being in a relationship with someone who had the same anatomical body parts as you. Our relationship was hot and cold from being in love one minute to feelings of hatred and rage the next! Eventually, the emotional rollercoaster took a toll on our relationship and we went our separate ways!

But now she was back, back in front of me, and truthfully, I was fine with it because I had no desire to be with a woman anymore! With no hesitation when my son died, she said, "I am on the way and she was there almost immediately! After the funeral, we remained in contact, which isn't unusual for me honestly. I keep in contact with the majority of my ex's and we all have healthy relationships. However, one day during a general conversation she says, "*Zanetta, I have to get something off my chest!*" I say, "*sure, what's up?*" She then says, "*I first want you to know that I've watched you from afar and I am so proud of you and the woman you've become. I am grateful to have you back in my life and I would never do anything to jeopardize that again!*"

It was what she said next that made me pause, "*but I have to be honest with you…I haven't seen you in 15 years and the moment I saw you in person, all my* emotions for you flooded back. I had no idea I was still in love with you after all this time!" I was shocked and had no idea because I thought we were just being friendly with one another. We kept checking on each other more frequently and before we knew it had started to become routine for the both of us! I found myself enjoying the routine!

I had been a single woman for twelve years and in no relationship. I was reeling from my son's death and very vulnerable and lonely. I had on a strong façade to live up to as a strong black woman. However, behind that public strength was a woman spiraling into the unknown and trying to learn to live without the beat to my heart. Jade asked me to come to visit her during her son's birthday weekend. I wasn't really sure if that was a good idea or not, but I said, "*yes*" even though I wasn't sure of myself or the situation that I was walking into. I still said, "*yes*." I was that character in the cartons that had the devil on one shoulder and an angel on the other shoulder. One part of me felt like destroying everything I had built. I wanted to destroy it because I felt like there was a small group of people that wanted to see if I would go back to my old lifestyle and fail. Then there was also this group of people looking to me as if I was superwoman. So, it was as if in one breath I wanted to destroy everything so they would see that I was human and flawed. In those moments, I would hear the Holy Spirit say, "this not going to happen!" I mean I could literally hear the Holy Spirit laughing on the inside of me. Then the Holy Spirit would say, "you're not going back it's not happening!" When I would hear the holy spirit, I became recharged like a battery and I knew that I would be ok and was free from bondage.

So, again against my better judgment, I went and I basically cried the entire weekend! She never touched me and I never touched her. Ironically, we had a good time…but yes, I cried the whole time. I cried because I was mad at myself for even having the thought and putting myself in that position knowing how vulnerable I was! But then at the same time, I also rejoiced knowing that even though I had dove into the rabbit's hole, I was still able to stand! My emotions were still all over the place!

Even though I made it out of that situation seemingly unscathed, I started watching porn! Now for some, that may seem normal, but not to me! Even as a kid or young adult, porn and masturbation were never my thing. So, as a woman of God that has never believed in living a double life, this was a major problem for me. I was so embarrassed, and I felt like a failure! The crazy thing was I would watch this stuff for hours because I had been suffering from insomnia since my son's death. I would stay up all night just going from video to video! What was even crazier was I had no history of masturbating, which made the entire situation even crazier. So, here I was watching porn not masturbating just fiending for more. This situation just puzzled me and I just didn't understand it!

Then on top of that, I began having panic attacks! I'd find myself on the floor disheveled and disoriented from a panic attack! I did my best to keep fighting, but I was hanging on by a mere thread. I felt as if one more tug and I was going to unravel. I had so much grief and anxiety began to overwhelm me. I would smile in everyone's face, but behind closed doors, my tears flowed incessantly. As a result, everyone kept telling me that I was so strong! If only they knew that I was sinking into a deep depression and temptation was knocking at my door. I finally mustered up enough courage to talk to Apostle about everything.

Take no part in the unfruitful works of darkness, but instead expose them.

-Ephesians 5:11- ESV-

5

My Alabaster Box
(timiotes, shemen)

After speaking with my Apostle
about all the strange occurrences, she
suggested I try therapy. As much as I
hated the idea of going to therapy, I
reluctantly found myself on the
therapist's couch. You see African
Americans have basically been
programmed into believing that people
do not need therapy. Some people
believe by doing so, we are deemed
crazy or weak and that is not the case.

Of course, the purpose of therapy is to talk about your issues, but I thought that we would be starting from "my present sufferings." I did not realize that we would be going back to the beginning of my inception to address every issue under the sun! This basically meant I had to hash up everything from my past...the abandonment of my birth father...how my mom was in and out of my life... how my stepfather never once told me that he loved me. No topic was off limits during therapy. I had family that I knew nothing about. I shared how I was molested by my uncle. I relived a lifestyle of being a borderline alcoholic. Of course, I discussed being a former homosexual. I talked about having to fight all my life… fighting depression, fighting anxiety, and f=fighting to live after several attempted suicides as a teenager.

And on top of all that, now I also had to address my (*after Christ*) issues. I confessed to the therapist that I was still trying to find out things about my identity. I revealed my vulnerability and fragility after my son died. The was so many changes. I was having panic attacks and losing people that I thought were friends. I overheard family having side conversations, even making wagers if I was going to stay saved and dedicated to God. It is funny because they talked about me before I changed my life and yet, I was still being talked about for changing. I was trying to find my way and figure out who I am after all the changes, just never felt valued. Then... the icing on the cake was losing the most important thing to me, my son! No one knows the cost of the oil in my Alabaster Box! NO ONE! Yet I had to address ALL of that!

I recall my very first therapy session the therapist dropped the biggest nuggets or should I say blessing on me. I was not losing my mind! I wasn't going crazy! I already knew that I battled depression and anxiety, but her words blew my mind. She said first Zanetta, one thing that I would diagnose you with is *"chronic trauma.",*

"Zanetta, because of all the trauma you've experienced through the years every traumatic experience left your brain bathing in a hormone called "cortisol" which is a stress hormone, and because of the loss of your son now your brain is drowning in

that same stress hormone. So, I said, *what is that? Explain it, please?*

She commences to tell me, "*from inception as your brain begins to grow you have memories even some that you will never remember, so basically every time something negative or positive happens, those memories are etched on your brain, and every time a negative memory is* etched *on your brain you produce "cortisol," again is the stress hormone."*

The therapist said, "*you have dealt with this throughout the years sometimes handling hit well and other times not so well hence the impulsive behavior."* She said, *"since being saved you've gained tools and knowledge to help you balance where you've been. Now that your son has been murdered, your brain is drowning in cortisol and you are reaching for anything you can to get a release."*

I thought that was the most profound information for me in this season. That conversation gave me a place to put a lot of things that I was dealing with in my life. It connected the past, present, and future. It gave me more ammunition along with my faith to fight strategically and pay attention to a few more things. I still could not understand for the life of me why I started watching porn! At this point, I had been abstinent ten years and had never masturbated during that time. I had not consumed alcohol and had no vices. Yes, I prayed, yes, I worshiped, but at times I need that release because now I knew the cortisol hormone levels in my head were so high, but I had no release valve. In other words, I had to find a healthy way to release the cortisol and increase my endorphins!

I kept praying and worshiping just doing my best to stay connected to God. I slowly added exercise the panic attacks subsided because working out became that release valve. I was able to cry, yell, scream and whatever I needed to do at that moment. I was able to do this in a completely judgment-free, safe environment!

> *There hath no temptation taken you but such as man can bear: but God is faithful, who will not suffer you to be tempted above that ye are able; but will with the temptation make also the way of escape, that ye may be able to endure it.*
>
> *-1Corithians 10:13-ASV*

Now that I found an outlet to keep my hormones in check, I had to address the fact that I had been slowly distancing myself from ministry. Embarrassment caused me to shy away and build up walls. I went before God in private which gave me strength to face the public.

6

Who Serves the Table
(Abodah)

I remember stopping at Apostle's house before heading to the funeral home to make arrangement for my son's funeral. I began to discuss the funeral I envisioned and details. I am not quite sure how it was said, but she went on to ask me if I wanted her to do the eulogy and I interrupted her, I said *"I'll do it!"* Some might ask why I would agree to such a thing.

Suppose one of you has a servant plowing or looking after the sheep. Will he say to the servant when he comes in from the field, '*Come along now and sit down to eat? Won't he rather say, 'Prepare my supper, get yourself ready and wait on me while I eat and drink; after that, you may eat and drink'? Will he thank the servant because he did what he was told to do? So, you also, when you have done everything, you were told to do, should say, 'We are unworthy servants; we have only done our duty.'*"

- Luke 17:7-10- NIV-

I said, "*I'll do it*" because I realized that in my son's untimely death…the table had been set! As I looked around at my family, I realized that the table had been set. As I looked at devastation on the faces of my son's friends, I realized the table had been set.

Despite how I felt, I was either going to sit at the table, spiraling l out of control and wallowing in my own sorrow. Instead, I made the exchange to serve at (*Abodah*) the table. Let me explain. I realized that the venom of the pain had to be extracted out because like in the 233rd Psalms, "*a table had been set in the presence of my enemies.*" Everyone needed to eat! The table was filled with the goodness of the Lord in the worst of situations. What was there to eat off that table? Those who sat could eat of the goodness of God, eat of God's mercy, eat of God's grace, eat of God's forgiveness, and most importantly, eat of God's love! His love and mercy were overflowing and ready to be devoured. You see many of the people that loved my son including family and friends didn't understand and know the nature of God!

Truth be told, many of them were killers, thugs, and drunks to name a few. Then there were others that dealt with other issues like hate, fear and unforgiveness! God gave me revelation that my job was not to sit at but serve the very table that I should by all accounts be stretched out on. The eulogy was my assignment by God. I decided to allow the world to see God's character, God's patience, God's forgiveness, and most importantly God's heart!

In the same way, let your good deeds shine out for all to see so that everyone will praise your heavenly Father.

- Matthew 5:16- NLT

7

I Am the Light

(Or)

Even though I was in the darkest place in my life and wanting to run away from my own shadow, I had to find inner strength to obey. Burying my child was the nightmare that no parent could prepare for or deserve. I felt like a boxer in the ring with my back against the ropes being pummeled by the enemy! Blow after blow, these hits were torment. I refused to hold on to what I saw with my natural eyes or felt in my mind. I had to lean into God even more and when I saw that dark, menacing shadow of the enemy, I saw God's light just began to shine through me. It became a beacon of light, hope, grace, forgiveness, and love. And by no means is this me tooting my own horn because I've had many days that I have been on my hands and knees crying out to God why? *"Lord, why did you let them take my only begotten son? You know that was my baby boy! God, they snatched my heart out my body and you expect me to keep living? Why?"*

God said, *"Zanetta, do you remember when you received the prophetic work saying, that Zanetta you are in the* fire...just like Shadrach, Meshach and Abednego and that there is a fourth person in the fire with you and that fourth person is Jesus?" I said, "yes I remember!"

King Nebuchadnezzar made an image of gold, sixty cubits high and six cubits wide, and set it up on the plain of Dura in the province of Babylon. He then summoned the satraps, prefects, governors, advisers, treasurers, judges, magistrates, and all the other provincial officials to come to the dedication of the image he had set up. So, the satraps, prefects, governors, advisers, treasurers, judges, magistrates, and all the other provincial officials assembled for the dedication of the image that King Nebuchadnezzar had set up, and they stood before it.

Then the herald loudly proclaimed, "Nations and peoples of every language, this is what

you are commanded to do: As soon as you
hear the sound of the horn, flute, zither, lyre,
harp, pipe, and all kinds of music, you must
fall down and worship the image of gold that
King Nebuchadnezzar has set up. Whoever
does not fall down, and worship will
immediately be thrown into a blazing
furnace."

Therefore, as soon as they heard the sound
of the horn, flute, zither, lyre, harp, and all
kinds of music, all the nations and peoples of
every language fell down and worshiped the
image of gold that King Nebuchadnezzar
had set up.

At this time some astrologer,[1] came forward
and denounced the Jews. They said to King
Nebuchadnezzar, "May the king live
forever! Your Majesty has issued a decree
that everyone who hears the sound of the
horn, flute, zither, lyre, harp, pipe, and all
kinds of music must fall down and worship
the image of gold, and that whoever does not

*fall down and worship will be thrown into a
blazing furnace. But there are some Jews
whom you have set over the affairs of the
province of Babylon – Shadrach, Meshach,
and Abednego – who pay no attention to
you, Your Majesty. They neither serve your
gods nor worship the image of gold you have
set up."*

*Furious with rage, Nebuchadnezzar
summoned Shadrach, Meshach, and
Abednego. So, these men were brought
before the king, and Nebuchadnezzar said to
them, "Is it true, Shadrach, Meshach, and
Abednego, that you do not serve my gods or
worship the image of gold I have set up?
Now when you hear the sound of the horn,
flute, zither, lyre, harp, pipe, and all kinds of
music, if you are ready to fall down and
worship the image I made, very good. But if
you do not worship it, you will be thrown
immediately into a blazing furnace. Then
what god will be able to rescue you from my
hand?"*

Shadrach, Meshach, and Abednego replied to him, "King Nebuchadnezzar, we do not need to defend ourselves before you in this matter. If we are thrown into the blazing furnace, the God we serve is able to deliver us from it, and he will deliver us[c] from Your Majesty's hand. But even if he does not, we want you to know, Your Majesty, that we will not serve your gods or worship the image of gold you have set up."

Then Nebuchadnezzar was furious with Shadrach, Meshach, and Abednego, and his attitude toward them changed. He ordered the furnace heated seven times hotter than usual and commanded some of the strongest soldiers in his army to tie up Shadrach, Meshach, and Abednego and throw them into the blazing furnace. So, these men, wearing their robes, trousers, turbans, and other clothes, were bound and thrown into the blazing furnace. The king's command was so urgent and the furnace so hot that the flames of the fire killed the soldiers who took up Shadrach, Meshach, and Abednego, and these three men, firmly tied, fell into the blazing furnace.

Then King Nebuchadnezzar leaped to his feet in amazement and asked his advisers, "Weren't there three men that we tied up and threw into the fire?"

They replied, "Certainly, Your Majesty."

He said, "Look! I see four men walking around in the fire, unbound and unharmed, and the fourth looks like a son of the gods."

Nebuchadnezzar then approached the opening of the blazing furnace and shouted, "Shadrach, Meshach, and Abednego, servants of the Most High God, come out! Come here!"

So, Shadrach, Meshach, and Abednego came out of the fire, and the satraps, prefects, *governors, and royal advisers crowded around them. They saw that the fire had not harmed their bodies, nor was a hair of their heads singed; their robes were not scorched, and there was no smell of fire on them.*

Then Nebuchadnezzar said, "Praise be to the God of Shadrach, Meshach, and Abednego, who has sent his angel and rescued his servants! They trusted in him and defied the king's command and were willing to give up their lives rather than serve or worship any god except their own God. Therefore, I decree that the people of any nation or language who say anything against the God of Shadrach, Meshach, and Abednego be cut into pieces and their houses be turned into piles of rubble, for no other god can save in this way."

Then the king promoted Shadrach, Meshach, and Abednego in the province of Babylon.

-Daniel 3-

So, I had to put before me that no matter what was happening, God was with me through it all. He had not abandoned or forsaken me. That became my light in a dark place!

8

Revelation

(Apokalupsis)

In the last eleven years, I definitely saw the imprints of God's hands on my life. I was that butterfly that thought my life of darkness would be my demise, but God used it as my place of preparation. Simply put, I have come a long way from the out of control and perverse place.   I was no longer that scared 31-year-old that I wouldn't even call a woman because I was still an immature child in so many ways. I'll just say this scared 31-year-old girl, that had no idea about where she was headed in life before Christ intervened in my life. When Christ penetrated every form of darkness in my life, an exchange took place. I surrendered darkness for his redeeming light. I was transformed inwardly, and my outer appearance began to match what God was doing inside me. Like a metamorphosis of a caterpillar into a butterfly, in the loss of my former identity, I gained wings that allowed me to soar. I was gifted the power to rise above every poor decision and even tragic circumstances of my past. These are some of the declarations, scriptures and affirmations that strengthened and empowered me to navigate on my journey in my deliverance process and they are not in any specific order:

> ➤ *Give it to God/Exchange your will for God's will for your life:*

I, (Zanetta) had to relinquish my control and give up my will for God's will. Truthfully, that not an easy thing to do! But I knew that if I hadn't tried something different the outcome could've possibly turned fatal, just as it had for my son! Often times, I get questioned on how did I change my life or how did I come out of homosexuality? I somewhat cringe at that question because people are always looking for a blueprint or manual on how things should happen. A lot of times when I tried to explain the process, people either do not believe me or I could not find the words that would penetrate to their souls. Hopefully, your heart and mind are aligned, and you can understand. I was tired and I knew that something in my life had to change. I had to give up something for a new way- (exchange). I surrendered my will for God's will, that's the first thing!

For we know that all things work for the best for those who love God, who also are called according to his purpose.

-Romans 8:28-

> ➢ *Faith without works is dead... how can you ever achieve your goals no matter what they are if you do not put in work?*

The second thing that I learned pretty quickly was faith without works is dead! Growing up, I was taught you pray about it and you let it go. When deliverance is taking place that is the farthest thing from the truth! Just like anything else in life, if you want something, you have to put in some form of work to get it, to make it happen, or to change it. I heard another pastor say it best; deliverance=work! For the most part, sin is sin, now there are stronger demons/strongmen, as well strongholds that present themselves the more you entertain sin and move farther away from God. However, after I said yes to Christ, it was as if God began allowing me to redeem my time, all the time that I wasted in my 20's and 30's. Why? Because I gave to God. I would give God my fear and he would give me peace. I would give Him my anger and he would give me back love and in that my dry dead bones were beginning to form life again. My countenance began to change and it was as if time just began to rewind the clock on my behalf. Though, please under no circumstance do I ever want you to think that this was or is easy because it is not and it will never be! Being a Christian and truly doing your best to serve God and being the best version of yourself. I refuse to lie to you or sugar coat it for you. The struggle is real, but the rewards are far greater! You have to put in the work on a daily basis to truly be able to be who God has called you to be.

Dear friends, do you think you'll get anywhere in this if you learn all the right words but never do anything? Does merely talking about faith indicate that a person really has it? For instance, you come upon an old friend dressed in rags and half-starved and say, "Good morning, friend! Be

clothed in Christ! Be filled with the Holy
Spirit!" and walk off without providing so
much as a coat or a cup of soup – where does
that get you? Isn't it obvious that God-talk
without God-acts is outrageous nonsense?

I can already hear one of you agreeing by
saying, "Sounds good. You take care of the
faith department; I'll handle the works
department."

Not so fast. You can no more show me your
works apart from your faith than I can show
you my faith apart from my works. Faith
and works, works and faith, fit together
hand in glove.

Do I hear you professing to believe in the
one and only God, but then observe you
complacently sitting back as if you had done
something wonderful? That's just great.
Demons do that, but what good does it do
them? Use your heads! Do you suppose for a
minute that you can cut faith and works in

two and not end up with a corpse on your hands?

Wasn't our ancestor Abraham "made right with God by works" when he placed his son Isaac on the sacrificial altar? Isn't it obvious that faith and works are yoked partners, that faith expresses itself in works? That the works are "works of faith"? The full meaning of "believe" in the Scripture sentence, "Abraham believed God and was set right with God," includes his action. It's that weave of believing and acting that got Abraham named "God's friend." Is it not evident that a person is made right with God not by a barren faith but by faith fruitful in works?

The same with Rahab, the Jericho harlot. Wasn't her action in hiding God's spies and helping them escape – that seamless unity of believing and doing – what counted with God? The very moment you separate body and spirit, you end up with a corpse.

Separate faith and works and you get the same thing: a corpse.

-James 2:14-26

➢ *Accountability:*

Something else that became very pivotal for me was accountability. I have always been a "people pleaser" when it came to those that I was closest with before Christ. On the other hand, after Christ that became a great asset in my walk. To explain, I developed relationships with people that not only checked on me, but those same people I did not want to disappoint them. As a result, it helped me keep my eye on the prize, knowing the positive effect it would have on my son, my family, my ministry, and my readers.

Therefore, confess your sins to one another and pray for one another, that you may be healed. The prayer of a righteous person has great power as it is working.

-James 5:6

> ➤ *Power of the tongue, speaking the right things i.e., life and not death:*

I became cautious with my words... because there is the power of life and death in our tongues. All my life, all I heard was "you look like a boy, you act like a boy." At some point, I took on that

Identity and allowed other people's views and opinions of me to fester and grow. I gave my life to God almost eleven years ago and I have probably been delivered from homosexuality for about 7-8 years now. Shockingly, it was not until a recent photoshoot that I saw a reflection of a beautiful woman, a lady in the mirror and that all came from what had been spoken to me as a child. So, parents, friends, family whoever, be mindful of what you speak. They often time say words do not hurt but that is a lie conceived in the pit of hell! As a child, I cut my leg open on an exercise bike and needed stitches...truth is where the cut was located and how wide it was, they probably should've stitched me with dissolvable stitches on the inside and then stitch the outside, but they didn't. Years later, I would touch the scar and amazingly, I could still feel the tenderness on the inside of that cut. It had not healed completely even though many years had transpired. The moral of the story is…some wounds cut so deep that they never heal…not unless you serve a true and living God!

The tongue has the power of life and death." The stakes are high. Your words can either speak life, or your words can speak death. Our tongues can build others up, or they can tear them down.

An unchecked fire doubles in size every minute.

-Proverbs 18:21-

➢ *Change your people, places, and things:*

Sometimes you must change your company, surroundings, and habits. If you are walking out of your deliverance process, this is imperative for anyone no matter their struggle! How can you change your life if you are always in the same circles around the same people doing the same things...you may do ok for a while but at some point, it is going to overwhelm you and you're going to give in? It's unfortunate but we oftentimes think we are strong enough or strong-willed enough to face things that God didn't necessarily tell us to face at that time! There may come a time when you can or that time may never come but either way that is ok. For your safety and priority while walking out your deliverance process, steer clear. If God has an assignment for you in that area, he will make it apparent. He will certainly let you know...but only when the time is right...again in his time. I know what you are going to say. This is all I know; these people are all I know, and I am just supposed to turn my back on them? To me it often seems like everything about how who we are as people can be a gift and/or a curse...this was a big one for me because loyalty trumped a lot of things for me and sometimes that was good and sometimes it was a hindrance. I allowed myself to be in a potion that God did not want me in or put me in and now I had to fight to get back to where he had me, not where I put myself! The truth of the matter is some people are leaves, some people are branches, and some people are roots. We like to make everyone our roots and they are not, and you learn to be ok with that. It is like the saying that people come in your life for a reason, season, or lifetime. At the end of the day, if the people in your life are real friends, they will respect who you are and where you're at and they will be there. Next, be ok with being alone and go through your healing process! This was an extremely hard one for me. I felt as if I had always been alone, but the flip side of that is, I was always in a relationship trying to fill a void that only God could ever fill. For the longest time, I would say, "well if I am delivered why do I often have the desire to go back to women? God would reply, 'Zanetta, that your familiar place, just like the dog that kept going back to its own vomit!"

> *They prove the truth of this proverb: "A dog returns to its vomit." And another says, "A washed pig returns to the mud."*
>
> *-2 Peter 2:22-*

Finally, I think I talked about this in my first book but I had to sit and see why I desired to turn back to that which I had spewed out of my mouth, my body, and my soul.

> ➤ *Be ok with being alone and go through your process of healing:*

I learned that the issue was not even about women, it was one about me having this romanticized view of what a healthy relationship looked like because I never really saw what a healthy relationship. I fantasized that it would be like I saw in movies. I was plagued by loneliness…I hated being alone and I would deal and or accept just about anything, too hot have that feeling…no different than a drunk that would go back to that bottle or that drug addict that would go back for any high. So, I had to deal with why I felt so alone and start embracing my time spent alone as a good thing and not as if I was somehow devalued because I had no one in my life. In doing so it has allowed me more time to spend with God which is actually what you are supposed to do while waiting on your God-ordained mate! The only validation that's needed comes for God and God alone!

> *But each of you has your own gift from God; one has this gift, another has that. Therefore, this bible verse on being single shows that you are at an advantage when it comes to serving God because you can devote yourself completely.*

> *-1Cor 7:7-8-*

➢ *Trust in your leadership:*

You must be able to trust those that have leadership over you! Everyone is not always privy to love where they serve. It is my option that if you cannot trust the leadership around you then you are in the wrong place plain and simple. I could never see myself somewhere I do not trust those that labor for me, unless that's just a ploy for you not to get free!

Obey your spiritual leaders, and do what they say. Their work is to watch over your souls, and they are accountable to God. Give them a reason to do this with joy and not with sorrow. That would certainly not be for your benefit.

-*Hebrews 13:17-19-*

➢ *Don't lie to yourself about yourself:*

My Apostle and her husband always said do not lie to yourself about yourself! If you cannot look in the mirror and say, I have a problem then the problem is you. As my Apostle has said on many occasions, I'd rather deal with a demon over a stronghold because a demon has to do what it's told…in the name of Jesus of course.

You have heard about Jesus and have learned the truth that comes from him.

- Ephesians 4:21-

➢ **Study your Word:**

You must study your word and learn the ways of God. How can you face anything spiritually if you don't have or know what tools are needed for the battle?

> *Study to shew thyself approved unto God, a workman that needeth not to be ashamed, rightly dividing the word of truth.*
>
> *-2 Timothy 2:15-*

➢ **Walk out the word daily/ Be intentional:**

Next, be intentional. God requires us to not only read his world, but live his word.

> Don't copy the behavior and customs of this world, but let God transform you into a new person by changing the way you think. Then you will learn to know God's will for you, which is good and pleasing and perfect.

-Romans 12:2-

And on top of all of that here's a few more tips. Make sure that you put first things first, our God can be a jealous God and he wants nothing and I do mean nothing before! As you progress in your walk studying "generational curses" will be a most effective tool in your deliverance as well as studying the "Courts of Heavens." You can go back to my last book, "The Weight in the Wait" to learn a little more about those two things! Lastly, stay in His presence and worship! Worship, worship, worship Him in spirit and truth!

> ## *Identify and uproot your strongholds*

A stronghold is a place that has been fortified to protect it against attack. A place where a particular cause or belief is strongly defended or upheld. You see the thing about strongholds they can and most definitely will at some point even though you probably created them to protect you what actually did was create a false narrative. In this case, after identifying your stronghold it's your job to break and tear down those strongholds!

Resist him, firm in your faith, knowing that the same kinds of suffering are being experienced by your brotherhood throughout the world. And after you have suffered a little while, the God of all grace, who has called you to his eternal glory in Christ, will himself restore, confirm, strengthen, and establish you. To him be the dominion forever and ever. Amen.　　　　　　　　*-1 Peter 5:9-11*

9

I Am the Clay

(Kla)

If you haven't guessed it by now,
God is the "Potter" and we are the
"clay!" Clay is just clay and it can't
mold itself. But the thing is like I
said earlier, as the clay we have to
submit to His will because He is
the potter and He is matchless!
And without God, the clay is
useless and holds no value. God
is patiently taking time to shape
us, mold us, make sure we are
balanced and positioned correctly

because He alone has the perfect plan for our lives. This means that our lives and our future aren't left up to chance or fate and that God has the perfect plan for our lives.

For the last eleven years, I have been on His wheel. As a matter of fact, it probably goes back even farther, I just can't recall because of all the mess I was in! Just know that God has been shaping me and molding me into who He wants me to be with a firm grip like a potter holding his clay. I have been broken into a million pieces time and time again sometimes at my own hand, sometimes at others, and sometimes just by life! The enemy has tried to destroy me! He took my innocence and tried to whisper lies about my identity. I have had to fight family battles and cast down generational curses. He has tried to take my mental health through anxiety, depression, panic attacks and programming through porn. The enemy even tried to destroy my physical health through sickness and disease. My character has been put to the test time and time again. Finally, the most devastating and horrific attempt was the murder of my son which the enemy thought would annihilate my relationship with my savior. My son is gone! However, I refuse to get off the potter's wheel because what he has for me is far greater than the challenges and pain I have endured in this world. I have so much to look forward to including seeing my son again! I know that God is good and that He is faithful and sovereign. That is what I hold onto, while He perfects great and mighty works in me! Until I hear him say, "Well done thy good and faithful servant!" I will willingly be the clay!